Paul Ferrini's books are the most important I have read.
I study them like a Bible.

ELISABETH KÜBLER-ROSS

Paul Ferrini's writing will inspire you to greater insights
and understandings, to more clarity and a grander resolve
to make changes in your life that can truly change the world.

NEALE DONALD WALSCH

Paul Ferrini is an important teacher in the new millenium.
Reading his work has been a major awakening for me.

Iyanla Vanzant

Paul Ferrini is a modern day Kahlil Gibran— poet, mystic,
visonary, teller of truth.

LARRY DOSSEY

Paul Ferrini reconnects us to the Spirit Within,
to that place where even our deepest wounds can be healed.

JOAN BORYSENKO

Book Design by Lisa Carta

Sculptures by Antonio Canova (1757-1822)

Cover, pg. 135; Amor and Psyche, Louvre, Paris

Cover, pg. 70; Amor and Psyche with Butterfly, Louvre, Paris

Pp. 6, 119; The Three Graces, Woburn Abbey, Buckinghamshire

Pp. 13, 23; Hebe, National Gallery, Berlin

Pp. 28, 41, 127; Atoning Magdelena, Palazzo Bianco, Genoa

Pg. 33; Hercules and Lichas, Louvre, Paris

Pp. 62, 121; Stele for Angelo Emo, Museo Storico Navale, Venice

Pg. 88; Kenotaph for the House of Stuart, St. Peters, Rome

Pg. 78; Venus Italica, Palatina Gallery, Florence

Pg. 109; Psyche with Butterfly, Blundell Hall, Lancashire

Library of Congress Card Number 2001089511
ISBN # 978-1-879159-47-1

Manufactured in the United States of America

DANCING
with the BELOVED

Opening our hearts to the lessons of love

PAUL FERRINI

Table of Contents

Introduction

Dancing with the Beloved captures some of the nuances and the insights that came to me as one important relationship in my life ended and the seeds of another one were sown. This book also includes a number of my recent poems that, I hope, will provide an emotional complement to the prose narrative.

I have always learned more in my intimate relationships than in any other area of my life. Some of these lessons have been difficult and painful, but in the end they have always helped me to open my heart.

One of the most important things that I have learned about the nature of love is that it requires our trust. We need to trust ourselves. We need to trust our partner. And we need to trust in the inherent order and goodness of life. Lack of trust in any of these areas undermines our relationships and makes it impossible for us to penetrate the veil of fear that separates us from each other.

Trust, of course, is based on acceptance. We simply can't trust a person we don't accept. The attempt to do so is, I am afraid, one of the most frustrating aspects of relationship.

In my experience, few people understand what acceptance is. Or perhaps they understand acceptance in relative terms: they accept some things about their partner, but not others. Unfortunately, partial acceptance cannot give birth to trust. And without trust, love is infantile and selfish. Indeed, to call it love is really to misname it and trivialize its meaning.

If we want to experience love, we need to embrace our partner fully. We must be willing to let our partner be, just as s/he is. That means no fixing, no saving, no remaking of our partner to fit our pictures or anyone else's (including those of our parents or our friends).

That doesn't mean that we think our partner is perfect. We don't idolize him/her or close our eyes to his/her weaknesses. We simply see these imperfections for what they are and accept them as part of the total picture.

Such an integrated view is not fashionable these days. Dissection and analysis of our partner's weaknesses (and perhaps our own too) are the norm in many relationships.

The inability to see and hold our partner's wholeness is symptomatic of our inability to see and hold our own. Most of us have a deeply divided and antagonistic relationship with ourselves. This inner division, of course, plays itself out in every intimate relationship we have. It translates directly into neurotic thoughts/emotions and ambivalent behavior toward our partners.

Is it any wonder that our intimate relationships often fall apart? When both people lack confidence in themselves and are ambivalent toward each other, how can committed love be possible?

The truth is, it is not possible.

The truth is that our soulmate cannot come into our lives until we learn to like and accept ourselves warts and all. Moreover, our soulmate is as imperfect as we are. If we see his/her imperfections as obstacles to our love and acceptance, we will not break through the veil of our own fear.

Love is really an inside job. It starts in our own hearts and then expands to include others.

So it's time to stop focusing on the other person. It's not his or her fault that the relationship did not work.

It didn't work because we were unable to accept and to trust as much as the relationship required of us. We can focus on what the other person could not bring to the table, but that will not help us.

The issue is always what we are able to bring. Until we can bring all of ourselves, the person looking back at us will never meet our expectations.

And so the circle of love continues to move. Round and round the rosy. Pocket full of posy. Ashes, ashes. We all fall down.

We fall into the depths of despair, wondering if the desire for love and union is just a cross that we bear until the moment of our final crucifixion. . . . Yes, on the tail end of a relationship that does not work, the going seems a bit bleak.

But we must use our fall into despair to get grounded. We

must realize that love without acceptance is a non-sequitur. It doesn't compute now and it will never compute.

As long as two people need to change, improve, fix or redeem each other, the outcome of their relationship is quite predictable. It may begin with ballooning expectations that take both people up into the stratosphere, but it ends on earth where it began, often with a giant thump.

Maybe the next time we consider taking such a journey, we better consider a few basics, such as "do we really like the other person as s/he is? Are we okay with the fact that our partner washes only once a week and hasn't worked in four years? Are we able to deal with the fact that every other day our partner gets unspeakably angry for no apparent reason or is particular adept in the four Cs: constantly criticizing, correcting, and trying to control us?" And if the answer to these questions is "yes," maybe we might want to consider some form of emergency therapy!

Let's be realistic. Loving unconditionally is a great goal, but how many of us are ready to date Hitler's first cousin?

Of course, when we started dating him or her, we thought s/he was the Prince or Princess of Monaco, but we found out otherwise, didn't we?

What does it say about us if we keep choosing partners we can't possibly love and accept?

Maybe, once we have made contact with the ground, we

might want to consider choosing a partner we are capable of loving instead of someone we think has great "potential" to be our perfect lover.

Often this will mean looking at the contents behind the wrapper. What is the truth about this person? To what extent does s/he act and react based on fear and anxiety? And just as important: how skittish are we? Where do we exceed our own capacity to love four or fivefold?

If we are smart, we will keep both our eyes and our hearts open when we begin a relationship. Because, whatever we overlook in the beginning of a relationship—in ourselves or in others—we will have to face later on.

The truth will always come out. It can be disguised and hidden only temporarily. And it is not to our advantage to try to hide it.

Clothes do not make the man or woman. They just make an image that sooner or later will have to be destroyed if we want to see the real person.

In fact, the truth is that some people look better than they are and others are much better than they look.

If you don't know this yet, better learn it before you get back on the merry-go-round.

The truth about your soulmate is that s/he is just as good as you are. And the same is true about the partner you just broke up with.

Not better. Not worse.

Whatever is inside of you will come out. And one day, you will look at it and say "It's okay. I can live with that." And that will be the day your soulmate arrives.

I give thanks to all of my lovers and friends who helped me to learn what I needed to learn. May they embrace their true nature and the true nature of others. May they find peace and happiness. May they learn to give and receive love without conditions.

Namaste,
Paul Ferrini

Epiphanies

And of the light
that has led me
softly to your doorstep,

the light falling
through the branches
of the trees

at dusk,

the light
dropping
into shadow,

or following the fingers
of your hands
on the piano

into silence:

it is more than
the dwindling
of the day,
more than the end
of a journey.

It is harvest time
for the heart:
epiphanies

of heaven and earth,
male and female
joining together.

It is the hour
of our surrender.

Life is not Perfect

We want life to be perfect, but it is not perfect. It is imperfect, ragged, unfinished. It never seems to be the way we want it to be.

Life resists our expectations and our need for control.

Sometimes life appears inscrutable, even disorderly. It isn't really, but its meaning and order are often subtle, hidden, slow to reveal themselves.

Its order is not our order. What it seems to offer does not seem to match what we want. And we are impatient. We want to impose our order, our will. We want our expectations met, now!

"Get off it," life is constantly telling us. "No matter how hard you try, you aren't going to get what you want when you want it."

Life is constantly asking us to make adjustments, to give up our agenda. It is asking us to give up the conceit that we know the way things are supposed to be.

"Just let things be the way they are," it tells us, "and you will take the first step in the dance."

Letting things be is a way of saying to God "I'm willing to dance with you. You aren't a perfect God and you don't fulfill my fantasies or meet my expectations, but I can accept your reality the way it is."

If you have a life partner, you probably say the same thing to him or her.

You join in the dance, imperfect as it is.

You allow the raggedness of life to be what it is. You allow for the possibility that order will emerge in its own good time. You stop trying to force life to meet your terms and conditions.

You say: "It's good enough as it is. It is acceptable just the way it is right here, right now."

That's the moment of surrender, when you stop trying to control life, when you get off your ego trip.

Taoists know that when you let life be, it is thoroughly magnificent. In fact, it is magnificent even when you are trying to control it, but you can't see the magnificence, because you are fighting "what is."

The Taoist says: "Give up the fight. Surrender to what is. Jump in the river and let the current take you. If you must swim, swim with the current, not against it.

Don't oppose life. Work with it."

When people ask you how things are, just tell them "Life is bizarre and unpredictable, but I'm working with it."

You don't have to agree with life to be present in it. You don't have to agree with God, or your partner, or your parents, or the Dow Jones average to be a happy player.

A happy player plays because playing itself is the magic.

Each moment is a chance to play happily. Can you play happily, even though life isn't showing up the way you want it to?

Job lost his family, his possessions and his health, but he still said "I'm hanging in there, God, even though you sure are trying my patience."

God rewarded Job, not because he was obedient, but because he was patient. Give life time to reveal itself and it eventually does.

The meaning is always there, but you don't always see it when you want to.

When you surrender, that's when the meaning becomes clear to you. When you let go, then you see the gift God wants to give you.

There is always a gift being offered you, because life is inner perfection revealing itself gradually in form. You just have a hard time seeing the nature of that perfection because it doesn't match your immediate wants and expectations.

That was the reality Job was living in, and it is no less ours: Consciousness is always in a crisis of faith. It knows that something hidden is revealing itself, but it can't see it or touch it.

Faith means knowing the gift is there even when it is invisible and intangible.

Faith, patience and humor are the ingredients of a great dance. But this dance can't happen until you give up your need to know or to control. In your proud, unsurrendered state, all you can do is step on people's toes.

You have to surrender what you think you know and relax into the moment. Then, the dance can begin.

Faith is a gesture of consciousness. It is not an existential reality.

One person may have faith and another may not. One person may surrender and another may seek to control.

But the truth for each is the same: Try to control and you lose control. Trust and you come into alignment with the greater Will.

Do you want to dance the great dance or not?

It's up to you. God doesn't care whether you dance or not. S/He is not invested in the choice you make.

If S/He were, S/He'd be as miserable as you are. No, God doesn't give a flying fandango what you decide to do.

That's the surrender S/He made when you were given free will. God said "Let people decide and learn from their mistakes. I will not control them or rescue them."

That's God's gift to you. It doesn't seem like much, but it is really an awesome gift.

Give that gift to any one of your friends and see how powerful it is. Just tell them "I love you and I support you in making your own choices. If you make a mistake, I'm not going to jump in and try to fix you, because I trust that you will learn from it."

Try it and see how powerful it is.

So that is the gift that God gave to you.

Are you ready to dance yet?

If not, rest assured it's okay. You aren't going to be punished. You can join the dance whenever you are ready.

God gave you plenty of time to make up your mind.

There's no rush.

Just remember, you aren't dancing with a perfect God, any more than God is dancing with a perfect human.

Because the dancers are imperfect, the dance appears awkward at times. But when the dancers forget about their imperfections and surrender to the dance, it has an unexpected grace.

At times, it is luminous.

That's what happens when we surrender our little will to the greater Will. That's what happens when we forget who we are as separate entities and become dancers in the dance.

We could not achieve this grace if we were trying to obtain it.

Thank God for hiding it in the dance where we can discover it, but we can't tamper with it.

Grace is round and open, like the dance. It comes from an unknowing, not from a knowing.

Knowledge is a double-edged sword. It may give power to the one who wields it, but it cannot bring peace. It cannot bring us to the round table.

As Rumi said, the door that separates the two worlds is round.

Life is a circle. It doesn't matter whether you are inside it or outside it.

What say you, dear brother or sister? Are you ready to dance?

Do you Recognize me Now?

Can you be completely one with me
and still come back to yourself?

Can you live in our surrender
and carry it back and forth
between the world of time
and the world where time does not exist?

Can you live on the undefended edge,
where the breezes of love blow
not just for a day or a month or a year,
but for an eternity?

Can you be defined by that wave
into which our two waves merge?
Can you live in its trajectory
and die in its embrace?

Many men have asked you to dance,
but has anyone asked you to dance like this?

With or without bodies, it does not matter!

Will you be all that you are in its fullness
and let yourself spill over into me?
Will you harvest your tears with mine
and water the ground with them?

Will you bring me into the secret caves
of your doubts and your fears,
allowing the moonlight to guide us
through the snowy woods?

You have come to me from deep waters,
ascending from the center of the circle.

Now as I dance, moving around the circle
from one partner to the next,
I once again await the depth of your eyes
and the electricity of your hand.

But I am lucky that the dance ends
before we come face to face.
I know when that moment comes
I will be lost forever, and so will you!

You see, I am not just the one
who comes to you in the dance. Rumi says:
"Lovers don't finally meet somewhere.
They're in each other all along."

Do you recognize me now?
Rumi says: "Gone inner and outer,
no moon, no ground or sky."
Has anyone asked you to dance like this?

Dancing with the Pain

"Impatiens are the only flower that will grow in the shade," you told me, busily filling up the old planters with soil and hanging them on the hooks above the railing on the front porch.

You even turned the old teapot—the one we left on the stove and forgot about—the one you meticulously scrubbed to remove its black, charred residue—into a flowering planter.

Martha Stewart would have been proud, except that the teapot looked a little small for the step you put it on . . . Oh well, the flowers would grow. In time, they would earn a more generous place at the entrance to the house.

Now I cannot think of you without waves of pain sweeping through my body. It is so intense I think I am going to throw up or pass out.

Hearing your voice on the phone helps, but I'm afraid it's just another trough in the swell of oncoming waves.

I don't want to say goodbye. I don't want to give up the lifeline of your voice, but I know that I can't hold onto it.

"There is room for love even when the heart is breaking," you told me, and I know that you are right.

I have never loved you more than I do now.

It is amazing to me how here, at the edge of the abyss, there can be such tenderness.

We are like two wounded warriors dying on the battle-field, our hands reaching out to touch before the last breath is taken.

You told me that you were coming here to learn to take your armor off. Now, I can't help notice that you went down wearing it, and so did I.

The morning after you left, I went outside and noticed that you had finally found a place that works for the old teapot. In a corner of the porch, near the stairs, you had made a pile of the rocks you gathered on the beach and placed the teapot with its red flowers on top.

Now when I enter the house, I am greeted by a beauty that was not here before.

I know this is the gift you wanted to bring. And I am happy that I can receive it now.

Now the entrance to the house is graced with red flowers that grow even in the shade. Here, a little light goes a long way.

Before you left you told me that you were overwhelmed by the intensity of my love for you.

You needed the shade too.

You had to put 3,000 miles between us to be able to receive the gift I had for you.

Well, at least we are holding hands at the edge of the abyss. . . . Too much anger. Not enough skillfulness in own-ing it.

Can we learn to own it at a distance and then dance closer, or is the dance over? Will our anger keep overpowering our love, or will we learn to love each other through our anger?

Little boy and little girl pushing Mommy away, because Mommy's love isn't safe.

Mommy's angry. So don't get close.

"Mommy found fault with me," you tell me "and I find fault with you. I can't seem to stop it. The least little thing triggers my anger. And you can't deal with it. . . . You are afraid of my anger. You don't stand your ground. Then I feel abandoned."

"I know," I say. "We keep going round and round in circles."

"I know it may be too much to ask for," you finally admit, "but I need a Shaman to stay with me while I rage out."

"I'll try," I say, totally ingenuous. "Go ahead a put the lion with the sheep."

"Won't work," you warned. And you were right. As soon as the lion began to roar, the sheep got a train ticket to New Zealand.

Neither you nor I know how to lie next to the lion without running away or roaring right back.

Only a very secure sheep can lie with a lion.

Here, at the well, at the entrance to the abyss, can you look at your anger and not give it to me? Can I stay present with you when you are angry without pushing you away, even though your anger scares me?

Can I be with my fear and face your anger, realizing that it is just a reflection of my own?

Can either of us be with the other person's judgment or anger without reacting?

Is it too much to expect?

The nature of love is that it brings everything that is not love to the surface.

There's no way around it. That's the dance.

Changing partners does not help. Leaving your partner does not help.

The dance continues, no matter who is dancing. It strips away all illusions. It is completely devastating.

When it is over, all you have is love.

There is no more resistance, no more struggle, no more pain, no more pushing or holding back.

You are just a leaf floating in the river. You move with the current. You do what love tells you to do.

Fearing for my Life

Meeting you,
I shuddered,
fearing for my life.
Now I understand why.

Death has come
in the guise of the beloved.
The one I used to be
is gone forever!

Submitting to Love

It is not easy for us to submit to something more powerful than we are. We must, in a sense, be forced to do so.

We must recognize that we are no match for the current of the river. The pain of resistance is more than we can bear.

There comes a time when we realize that we have no choice. We must submit.

We think that we consciously choose the people we love, but that is a great illusion. The people we love are brought into our lives because they are our perfect mirrors.

If we choose them, we choose in a soul realm where there is no duality. And here we must face the choices we made there.

We must submit to the lesson being offered. If we squirm and wiggle, trying to avoid the lesson, it comes back later with more urgency.

Truth will not let us hide from ourselves or each other.

You see, it does not matter who our partner is. If we reject one partner because s/he is too difficult for us, the replacement is likely to be even fiercer.

Sooner or later, life will bring us a mirror we can't avoid or reject.

So we need to stop being stubborn. We need to learn the

lesson when it is in front of us, instead of finding fault with the mirror and looking away.

Progress on the spiritual path has to do with softening our rough edges. It means taking responsibility for our anger and our fear and not dumping them on someone else.

The armor has to come off or it kills us.

People have tried to dance with their armor on, but it doesn't work.

It doesn't work for them and it doesn't work for anyone else.

We need to find the place where we are vulnerable and learn to accept it and let others see it.

We need to soften into our humanness and be imperfect, incomplete, ragged, unfinished.

We need to stop pretending to be invincible when we feel like a total mess. We need to let ourselves be a mess.

We need to be as we are.

There is no one we need to impress. There is no one here we need to answer to or seek approval from.

Or if there is, we must not hesitate to disappoint him or her.

Sometimes there is no difference between a suit of armor and a three piece suit. We can't always look nice. We can't always look the part, much less play it.

It's time to wake up and look into the mirror. Before

reaching for the make up, we need to look at the eyes tired from little sleep, red and irritated from too much crying.

That's the way it is. We need to stop covering it up.

It won't stay that way forever.

Healing takes time. Feeling the pain is part of the healing and the learning.

Push pain away and it goes underground. It becomes chronic.

We need to be with the pain and let it take us back and forth from the place where the pain begins to the place where it ends.

All emotional states are a necessary part of the journey. If we have the courage to accept them, they can help us come more fully into our hearts.

The Funeral

"He's more than a friend," you told me
over a month into our relationship,
"and not sleeping with him
does not solve the problem."

"You need to find out
what that's all about
before our love can have a chance,"
I said with trepidation.

But it was a cruel decision.
It wasn't easy to undo
what had been done, to stop living
in the consciousness

that held us in the same fragile
but seamless body.
"You sound depressed," my friends said,
and, in a way, they were right.

Something in me was dying then
and I was left alone to bury the body.
You did not play the piano
at the funeral. Indeed, the event itself

seems to have slipped your mind.
But I have made my peace with all that.
I come here now from time to time
to plant flowers and remember.

Building the Foundation

We want the foundation of our love to be perfect, but it is not going to be. No foundation is perfect.

When I was building the post and rail fence I put up in the front yard, I started with a very clear plan. My friend helped me cut each post to the desired length with his chain saw. Then I got my posthole digger out and began to dig the eighteen inch holes to receive the posts. The first one was hard digging. I had to pull out rocks and maneuver around roots, but eventually I reached the desired depth and put the first post in.

The next hole went much faster. There were no rocks or roots to deal with. As a result, the first section of fence went up easily. I felt quite encouraged. I thought to myself "This is going to go up quickly, and I'll be able to do some other things today."

Well, that was not to be. The third hole was impossible. Nine inches down, I hit roots that were three or four inches thick. There was no way that I could cut through them. I tried moving the hole forward, backward and to the sides, but I couldn't avoid the roots.

Finally, I realized that I'd have to cut the post down. That wouldn't be easy—all I had was a handsaw. And I was worried that the post wouldn't be far enough into the ground to be stable. But there was no other option.

So I started to saw the post. I sawed all the way around it, but couldn't get the saw blade completely through. Finally, I had to whack the post against the pavement to get it to break. Fortunately, it broke off cleanly, and I set it in the hole.

It seemed to be okay and I thought "Well, if I just have to cheat on just this one hole, it will be okay."

But the next hole was just as hard. Twelve inches down I hit massive roots. So I had to get out my handsaw and start sawing again.

By then, my attitude was one of silent resignation. This was the only way that the fence was going to go up. Hopefully, it would be strong enough.

To my surprise and gratitude, the last hole went fairly easily and I was able to get the post a full eighteen inches into the ground.

As I put the final section of fence together, I realized that the three posts that needed to be most secure—the right angle post and the two end posts—had been buried a full eighteen inches. The fence was strong where it needed to be. And the middle posts—where I had cheated—were supported by the strength of the posts at the ends.

The fence looked beautiful and seemed plenty strong. It was a good fence, but hardly a perfect one. As in any building project, I had to deal with unanticipated obstacles and find a way to make things work with the conditions at hand.

You can have the most wonderful, intricate plan on paper, but as soon as you start to implement it, new factors surface that you hadn't taken into consideration.

Things always look better on paper than they do on the ground. Ideas are perfect in the abstract, but imperfect in the practical implementation.

That's just the way it is: Every project asks us to adjust our plan to meet the reality at hand.

Relationships are no different. We have a plan of the way we want them to go. But as soon as we start living with another person, new factors arise.

If we are smart, we revise the plan, so that we don't beat it to death.

We take the time to find out what each one of us needs and what the relationship needs. We see where each one of us must grow, stretch, compromise and adjust to be with the other person successfully, and where we just need to be accepted the way we are.

We see how we are imperfect partners for each other. We notice that there are needs the other person has that we can't meet now, and maybe not ever.

But we don't lose sight of where our foundation together is strong. We see where our love for each other is fierce and committed. We see where we are totally devoted to each other's joy and happiness.

We see our relationship as a work in progress. There are times when we wonder how we can possibly stay together. And there are times when we wonder how we could possibly live without the presence of the other person in our life.

This is the dance.

It's not a perfect dance. The abstract concept of our relationship always looks better than its practical, day to day reality.

In our ideal relationship, we don't hurt the other person and s/he does not hurt us. We are always understanding and supportive and so is our partner.

In our ideal, we don't get mad at each other. We don't rage at our partner as if s/he were an arch enemy, nor do we withdraw into a self-protective shell of denial and avoidance.

In our ideal, we are not judgmental or critical of our partner, nor is our partner judgmental and critical of us. In our ideal, we don't blame each other or punish each other for our mistakes. We don't want to reform, redeem or change each other.

In our ideal, our needs are not competing. We aren't afraid that we are going to sacrifice ourselves by being with our partner.

But in reality, all of this happens. We deal with anger, conflict, fear, shame, self-betrayal: you name it. Everything that we hope our relationship won't be we have to deal with.

That's the nature of the dance. Remember, the white knight is wearing a full suit of armor. And hidden in that armor are all his fears of intimacy: all his secret issues of abandonment and betrayal.

This is not true just for one knight or damsel. It is true for all.

We dance not just with the bright, cheerful, effervescent, trusting side of our mates, but with the dark, fearful, sad, angry and defensive sides.

If we aren't willing to dance with the dark side, the foundation never gets built. We never get to experience the fullness of love that we are capable of giving and receiving.

Until we accept our partner as the one we have chosen to dance with—until we stop lashing out and running away—we won't really know what the dance of intimacy is all about.

It is not a dance of ideal sentiments, but of longings and fears. It is a an evolving choreography where trust happens slowly and commitment is gradually earned.

Romance may open the door to love, but it does not help us walk through it. Something else is needed. Something deeper. Something a great deal more patient. Something ultimately more real.

The foundation of our love is not perfect and it will never be. In places, it is patched, fudged, jerry-rigged.

We wonder sometimes how it all holds together. Yet it does. It does because we want it to, because each day we are willing to do what the relationship asks of us, even if we sometimes do it kicking and screaming. It does because we keep dancing no matter what. We keep finding love, even as we move awkwardly and sadly through the pain. It does because we know and trust that our partner will be there for us, no matter what.

That is not something that we know right away. That is not something that we can promise in advance. It is something that happens in its own time.

It is the fruit of the journey, not the seed. To bear fruit, the seed must be planted and watered.

Difficult, challenging times must be weathered. Love must be strengthened beyond neediness and self-interest. It must die a thousand deaths to learn to rise like the phoenix beyond adversity of any kind.

It must be mistaken, wrong, unreasonable, stubborn, foolish, selfish, even cruel, so that it can see the depths of its error and learn from it.

Love is not a fragile, shiny thing, kept separate from the

pain and misery of life. It is born of our willingness to learn from our mistakes.

It is a jagged boulder thrown into the rushing stream, where it is assaulted and caressed, pushed and pulled by the current until its edges are smooth and yielding.

When you pick that smooth and shiny stone from the stream, do not forget what made it so complete in its surrender.

There is no one who learns to love without encountering the depth of her pain and her partner's pain.

That is the way it is.

In time we learn that all pain is the same pain. And we have compassion for our partners and for all the other human beings who suffer in the current of life.

In time, we learn to build our foundation as strong as we can and to celebrate it: to know that it is good enough, however ragged it seems; to know that stones we piled together here came from the river itself, and they have the strength and dignity of their journey, just as we do.

I Rest in a Certainty

There is no kind of lovemaking
that can express
the intensity of my love for you.

Try as I may,
I know these hands
cannot touch you

where you need to be touched:

beyond desire,
beyond pleasure,
beyond orgasm.

Yet I rest in a certainty
that I hold you there
in that unbroken embrace,

deeper than bodies go
and way beyond the time
these hands have to remind you

how deeply you are loved.

In Venice, above the Canal

I do not know who I am any more.

I have lost myself in your eyes.
I have fallen like a deep sea diver
into the smell of your body
lying next to mine.

I have lost my hands
to the sinews of your back,
my lips to your stomach,
and my tongue to the black hill
I climb when you arch your back
and your weight sinks
buttocks first
into my open palms.

Eroticism, you call it,
but I call it a tidal wave
and keep swimming until I dock
somewhere under your eyelashes,
or crash tattered sails and all
into the dark tunnel
of your left ear.

There was a time
when I thought it would be like this
but that time is so far away
it seems another life:

waiting for you by the school fence,
following you home,
sneaking into your room at night,
and rowing home at dawn
through the watery streets.

Reactivity

"Why didn't we do that?' you asked when I talked about just listening to each other without trying to fix anything, just listening so that we know what the other person is feeling. And sharing in a way that doesn't blame the other person for how we are feeling.

"I don't believe that we can do this process when our anger is up," I told you. "I think we need to cool off first. Otherwise, we can't hold the space for the other person, nor can we communicate in a non-blaming way . . . but you always want to go after it right away, even though you are upset."

"I have a hard time when you leave."

"Yes, I realize that now. I guess I hoped that you would see that I always come back."

"You come back and you've somehow reconnected to yourself and you are loving again with me, but I can't respond, because I'm still holding all that anger."

"I know. I can feel it. But I don't want to stand there and just let you blast me. It's scary for me to stand there when you are angry at me."

"That's where it all breaks down. We both have a problem dealing with the other person's anger. It's not safe for us to be angry at each other."

"Yes, I know that you're right. I don't feel safe when you get angry or critical of me. I put up my self-protective wall. I crawl into my shell. And if your anger is volatile, I have to get away from it. I have to leave."

"And I'm afraid to be angry around you. I'm afraid to say what I'm thinking to you for fear that you will react and run away. You are so sensitive to any negative thoughts or feelings that I have. You pick up on them right away. You ask me if I'm okay, but I'm afraid to tell you what is going on for me. And if I don't tell you, then it builds up and it explodes."

"I know that you would like me to be more able to sit with you when you are feeling unhappy or critical of me. But I have a hard time doing it. That's why I ask you to tell me how you are doing without blaming me. It makes it possible for me to understand and accept your experience. I can't do that when I'm feeling attacked."

"Well, I understand that. But I can't always find the right words when I'm upset. I just need to say whatever words come to me. And those words aren't always kind."

"No, they are often daggers."

"So don't you see . . . you can't accept my words because they are daggers and so I can't communicate with you when I most need to."

"I don't think that we should be trying to communicate

when we are angry at each other. We say things that we don't mean and we hurt each other."

"But, sweetheart, if you leave when I'm angry then I don't feel safe with you."

"Do you feel safer if I stay and defend myself?"

"Well, it's still hard, but it's not as hard, because I feel that you are trying to hang in with me. I feel more supported, even though it is not easy for either one of us."

"So you need to express your anger to me, no matter what, even if you are blaming me?"

"Yes, I think so. And I need to know that I can do that and you won't leave me. I need to know that you are strong enough to withstand my anger."

"I can see that. And I can see that it's really hard for me."

"I know it is. But I also know that we have to have enough safety in our relationship to be able to express our anger and know that the relationship can contain it. Also, it's not just me that needs to express my anger. You need to be able to express your anger at me too."

"I suppose that's true. Expressing anger is not something that feels safe to me, especially when it is mixed with criticism and blame, which seems to be the case 99% of the time. Plus, I believe that anger belongs to the person who is angry. I don't believe it is my responsibility to receive your anger or your responsibility to receive mine."

"Maybe not. In an ideal situation, each person would own their anger and face the pain and frustration behind it. That's what you would like, right?"

"Yes."

"But life isn't always like that. When we get angry, we project and blame. That's the reality. Are we supposed to just stop?"

"Yes, I think we need to just stop, and breathe and get space, and then come back and talk when we can own our anger without making the other person into a target for it."

"Well, I'd like to do that for you. But it isn't natural for me. I want to stay with what's happening. I don't want to stop. I want to get after what's bugging me. I want to get it all out on the table and look at it with you, but you seem to find that threatening."

"Yes, that's probably true. I guess I don't have faith that we can get after it without saying a lot of destructive things that we are both going to regret."

"You think the anger is obliterating, that it can't be contained or worked with?"

"Yes, I think so." But I also think that this is not just true for me. I think it's true for you too. We both have a problem being with the anger. You want to push it. I want to pull away. I think they are two sides of the same coin."

"Maybe. . . . so what do you suggest that we do?"

"Well, I think that I need to hang in there longer and see if I can work with you on it when the anger is up. And when I can't, I need to ask you for a break and hope that we can take an hour or two and look inside and "own" our feelings. Then, we can come back and create more of a ritual space, where each person is able to speak in an honest, but non-blaming way while the other listens without interrupting, so that we can really hear each other.

What do you think?"

"I think that would be good. I think we should try it. Maybe we could even try breathing together in silence while the anger is up to see if we both calm down. Would you try that?"

"Yes. I'd like to try that."

———————

This is the conversation we might have had if we had had enough trust in each other to turn the doorknob. Instead, we stood in front of the door and decided to back off because it wasn't opening.

The door isn't locked. It just isn't open yet. And it isn't going to open by itself. We are the ones who have to open it.

This is not Negotiable

After driving for two hours
I arrive to find the house empty.
A note tells me you forgot
you had an appointment:
"Make yourself at home.
See you at 10:30 PM."

I walk into the bedroom
and set my bag down
on the carved Haitian chest.
My ego says: You should leave.
You wouldn't have done this to her.
She doesn't deserve you."

On and on it goes.
I walk around the house
feeling sorry for myself,
trying to decide
if I should go or stay.

"I'm sad," I tell your parrot,
but he just stares back at me.
It is not the first time
I have thought
that I did not come first
in your life.

Suddenly, the door opens.
Your daughter runs in.
"I forgot my key," she says.
You come up the stairs cheerfully
and give me an affectionate hug.
"I came back just to kiss you,"
you say.

It isn't true, but it makes me
feel better anyway.
I look into your eyes
and can see that you feel
absolutely no guilt.

You depend on me to understand.
There is no place in this relationship
for my fears to get a foothold.

"Bye, Sweetie," you say,
heading back down the stairs.
"See you in a few hours."
"Well," I think, "now
I'll have to stay."

I sit down and pour myself
a glass of wine,
no longer feeling rejected.

I am not used to being loved
so fiercely, without even a hint
of sentimentality,
without any deference
to how I feel about it.

Facing the Shadow

Last night, I realized how important it was for you to tell me some of the things about me that you have difficulty with. Although I did not agree with many of your perceptions about me, I could see that you felt better being able to verbalize them.

In the past, I would have refused to hear what you had to say, because it was judgmental of me. I would have asked you to take responsibility for your judgments and not project your fears onto me.

But I understand now that such a stance on my part felt invalidating to you and caused you to feel that you could not share your thoughts and feelings with me. By insisting that you take responsibility for your fears and judgments, I succeeded only in silencing you.

That was not helpful to either of us.

I realize that I have difficulty with criticism. I have antennae that pick up critical vibrations from miles away. I hear even the tiniest inflection of judgment. I know when someone is making me a target of her own unresolved anger and self-judgment. I know when boundaries are crossed, and I am quick to point it out to whoever might be crossing them.

I want you to be responsible for your anger and your

pain. I want you to look at why something I say or do makes you frustrated, angry or uncomfortable.

But you don't want to look at what's up for you. You want to get after me.

And that scares me. So I tell you: "Only if you are responsible for your own anger will I be able to hear about it. If you make me the target of your anger, I will not stay and listen."

It never occurs to me that you aren't trying to abuse me. You are just not owning your own fear and your anger.

That might create the conditions in which abuse can happen, but it only becomes abuse if I buy into it.

I don't have to agree with your judgments. I can let you have them. I can know that they are about you and not about me and listen to whatever you need to say.

But that isn't what I do. As soon as I hear the judgment train coming, I bring my tanks out onto the tracks.

"Don't step over this line or I'll let you have it," I say.

I give you plenty of warning, or so I think. I think you have ample time to stop the train. But the train doesn't stop.

You keep coming at me. It doesn't matter that I tell you "please don't cross this line." Once you get going, you aren't going to stop. Indeed the very fact that I ask you to stop makes you more angry.

You don't feel that I am willing to hear you, and you are determined to "make me" hear you. You can't honor my boundaries, because you feel that my boundaries prevent you from being yourself.

So you keep coming. And I keep saying "Slow down, back off, or I'll let you have it."

And when you don't, I fire back. Indeed, I feel totally justified in defending myself.

And then I see what happens to you. I see that train lurch and groan and buckle and fall off the tracks. I see all that anger about needing to be seen crash and turn inward upon itself.

"Your anger is not my responsibility," I tell you. And I am right. But it doesn't matter.

You aren't going to come back for more. You feel defeated, scorned, betrayed and abandoned.

You aren't going to try again a little more consciously, owning your anger and judgments. You aren't going to tell me about your fears in a non-blaming way.

You are done. You aren't coming down these tracks again. "I can't be in a relationship with someone who doesn't allow me to express myself," you say.

It never occurs to you that you can "slow down" the train. It never occurs to me that I can get off the tracks and let the train run itself out.

You can be responsible for your thoughts and feelings, yet still share them with me. I can let you have your thoughts and feelings without needing to agree with them or defend myself from them.

There are ways to avoid a crash. Why aren't we able to find them?

We think we need to stand against the other person in order to stand up for ourselves.

It isn't true, but it is what we seem to believe.

We don't know how to remain friends when anger or hurt is happening. When we are triggered, we see an enemy, not a friend. We forget that we are on the same team. We forget that we both want the same thing from each other.

I forget that I have to be willing to forgive you for attacking me if I want to receive your love. Because your love isn't perfect.

You can't always love me the way that I want to be loved. You can't always respect my boundaries. You can't always take responsibility for your anger and judgments.

I need to forgive you for trying to give me your pain, your fear and your anger.

If I can't do that, I can't receive your love. And I know that you do love me, even though you do so imperfectly, raggedly, and awkwardly at times.

It is the same for me. I cannot always love you the way

you want to be loved. Sometimes I mistake your need to share your feelings with me as criticism of me and I blast you. I need your forgiveness for that.

My love is awkward and imperfect too.

My child and your child are so afraid of criticism. They're so afraid that they won't be good enough. They don't understand that they are okay just the way they are.

Your child does not need to get angry to be heard. My child does not have to avoid anger to hold onto himself.

We have a lot to learn together. We have only begun to understand the ground where we can meet.

"Sometimes I think that we are on different frequencies," you say.

"I don't think so," I say. "If we were on different frequencies, this train would have never met these tanks . . . we have the same lessons, the same wounds. The question is: are we willing to learn and heal together?"

"I don't know," you say. "I'm afraid the same thing will happen again. I'm afraid that we won't be able to do it and that I'll have to leave again. . . . I don't want to put you through that pain."

"I know," I tell you. "I'm afraid of that too."

A Virginal

Pieces of the hem of your dress
are scattered across the sky:
lavender in the soft gray light.

Dusk swims in the air:
soft pastels of salmon and rose,
tired wings yielding to the dark.

Your arrival is less certain than
the dark that follows day's end,
or the light that follows night.

Your ambivalence requires
contradictory outcomes
occurring at the same time

—earth wobbling on its axis,
uncertain whether to give birth
to night or day, light or shadow.

I know the formula you use:
If you are not needed, you will come.
Otherwise, you will stay behind.

Although you want more than
casual encounters,
you are afraid of being caught

by the pull of love
and placed in orbit
around a greater star.

I do not blame you for standing back.
Waking to the empty space
beside me,

I release you yet another time,
watching your footprints fade
as you climb the hills to the east

where light gathers red as blood,
inside the cavernous cover
of clouds.

Song of the Lover

I am the light
you seek,
bending like a vine
around each dark corner
of your life.

I am the water
that quenches your thirst,
the arms that embrace you
when you feel lonely
and neglected.

I am the love you hunger for,
the grapes
crushed underfoot.
I am the wine
made from your pain.

I am the lips
that kiss your tears,
and bear the weight
of the fist
that crushes your teeth.

I am the silence
made from your screams
of violation.

I am the one who tried
but could not love you
through his fear,
and I am the one
who washes your feet
and begs
your forgiveness.

I am the light you seek
in the blood-stained darkness
and the love
you hunger for
in vain.

I am the one
who has broken your heart
into thousands of pieces
and the one who brings balm
to the wound.

I am the son
who has nursed at your breast
and the mother
who has poured burning oil
on your lifted arm.

I have suffered and atoned
for each of
your transgressions.
I have bled and healed
from each of your wounds.

Though you have looked for me
in the passing eyes
of strangers,
I have never strayed
from your side.

Though you have run naked and bruised
through your dreams,
I have wrapped you
in the mantel of love
for all time.

Return of the Chariot

To ride the present is itself the chariot.

Will you ride with me,
not to turn back, but to love
without misgivings
for your pain or mine,

to dance with the sad wind
on ground zero,
mourning all the places in our hearts
spared and not spared?

Will you look into my eyes,
no matter what?

You, mother of intuition
and hopeless stars,
whose pain I know
beyond the bars of time or space,

you whom I courted
while the dark sky of youth
was dragged to death's
familiar altar,

you with whom I labor
long into night
till the day spins red and purple
into light,

you, the harbinger, the proof,
the reckoning,
the one whispering of light
at night's edge?

I have folded myself into your awnings.
Beware the swinging of the wind.

Mending the Torn Fabric

Sometimes I think that this time apart is about repairing the damaged vessel. We went into our union hard and quick, without really knowing each other. We put everything on the line before we were ready. I did not know what I was up against, nor did you.

Now we know. Now, we know what living together demands of us, and we realize we might have to work up to it. We might have to take the time to really learn how to communicate. We might have to learn to accept certain things about each other that we can't change.

We might need time to find intimacy in the places where we don't agree, where we don't connect. We might need to find compassion right in the middle of our judgments, our fears, and our thwarted expectations.

It is not easy to accept the reality of loving an imperfect person, a person who loves us back without being able to meet all of our needs.

We have to keep giving up our ideas of what we think love should be. Love is never that.

It is what is unfolding right now between us. It is the way we keep touching through our pain. It is the way we keep finding each other on the other side of our fear.

It isn't very romantic, but it sings with authenticity.

It is our creation.

It is not surprising perhaps that you could not fit yourself in to the rhythms of my life. I am sure that I could not fit myself in to your rhythms either.

We are looking at something different here: creating a rhythm together. It is what we do when we go walking together. I adjust my pace and you adjust yours. Walking hand in hand is different than walking alone.

It is a totally different discipline.

We are both used to walking alone. We are both good at having our own way, moving at our own pace.

But we haven't learned to walk hand in hand, step by step, with another. Not many people have.

To walk gracefully, both people must adjust, not just once, but countless times. The dance requires hundreds of tiny shifts in thought and feeling. It requires constant awareness of strain and awkwardness so that corrections can be made.

It means taking care of yourself and taking care of your partner. It means doing both equally well, not one better than the other.

You understand this. I know that you do.

But it is easy to lose sight of. It is easy to think "I'd rather just walk by myself" when an adjustment is called for. It is easy to bail out, sacrificing the relationship to some abstract ideal that will never be realized. But there is nothing abstract about living with another person.

The child understands this. The child feels the tides of emotion as they come and go. S/he is imprinted by innuendoes of wind and salt spray. She lives inside the footprints on the beach until the sea covers them over. S/he does not understand abstraction. S/he does not do well when a relationship ends because of some concept held in the mind.

The child just wants to be loved. And it is crucified again and again as the mind finds that it is incapable of loving this person or that one.

We need to take care of that child. We need to build a place for him or her to live safely.

We cannot do it with our minds, yet we need to use our minds to understand the scope of what must be done.

The mind must realize that union requires it to stretch beyond its familiar boundaries. Union requires it to go beyond "me" or "you" into a vague, scarcely understood and almost mystical place called "us." This synergy of mental and emotional landscapes happens through the mutual surrender of thoughts and feelings of separateness in your heart and mine.

It is a new consciousness being born. And it cannot be born as long as we hold onto separate agendas.

To think this is easy is to totally disregard our fear. We

are afraid to let go of our separateness. We are afraid of losing ourselves in the other person, afraid of not being seen or acknowledged, afraid to see a familiar aspect of ourselves dying into something much greater, more powerful, and completely unknown.

True relationship requires the death of ego. But ego cannot be sacrificed, on a cross, as it were, or it will return again and again, hungry and unfulfilled. It must be surrendered voluntarily, willingly and joyfully, and then it can be resurrected into something greater and more profound.

The caterpillar struggles inside the sac of transformation. First it puts out one wing, and then another. Surrender does not happen all at once. Dying and being reborn are simultaneous phenomena.

Is it so surprising that we are scared, that we are afraid of losing ourselves in our love for each other? Let us not underestimate the transformation that is being asked of us, nor the fear that comes up as the child reaches for the love s/he has always wanted and has never been able to give or receive.

Our wounds must be surrendered. Our armor must come off. Our love must lead the way, pulling our fear along with it. The caterpillar must enter the cocoon knowing that when it emerges it will no longer be a caterpillar.

Being a butterfly seems a romantic notion. But the

process of becoming a butterfly is anything but romantic.

It requires that we move through our fears. It requires that we face the unknown.

It means that we move toward the place where we meet without knowing what it looks like or how it will feel when we get there.

Union happens in a place beyond fear, a place of tenderness and safety. Yet it is difficult for us to find this place. The separate sense of self must die for the transcendent Self to be born.

One day the sun will rise above the horizon and you and I will be a single flower reaching for the light and the stillness of the air. Others will celebrate our beauty. Yet they will never know how we struggled on the brink of the abyss, afraid to let go, afraid to surrender into the unmistakable love that we share.

Friendship

I know that friendship is the bedrock of our relationship.

Friends do not spend every minute together, but they think of each other often. They check in with each other just to make sure that everything is okay. They are concerned about each other.

When friends get together, they have fun. They do things they both enjoy. They talk about their lives. They share their frustration and their joy.

Friends do not worry about what they don't share. They don't try to fix each other. They accept the other person as s/he is. That is the essence of being a friend: not to judge, but to accept, to understand and support, regardless of the situation.

That is what we do when we are apart. We are great friends.

And it is what we do a lot of the time when we are together. But then we push a little and we start to lose it.

Friends don't push each other. They give each other space. They respect each other's boundaries.

That's why friendships can last forever.

When people try to be lovers before they have learned to be friends, they are asking for trouble.

A friend shows you his pain, and you don't get threatened and attack or run away. You just hold your friend's pain with compassion.

You don't take it personally. You don't have to do anything about it. You just sit with your friend and offer understanding and support.

Lovers have a hard time doing that, because their pain is usually connected to their partner's pain. Lovers often feel attacked by each other's expectations and judgments. They frequently feel compelled to defend themselves or justify their behavior to each other. Is it any wonder that they have trouble listening to each other and being supportive?

That's why lovers have to call "time out." They have to learn to back off and give each other space. They have to learn to let the other person be and respect his or her boundaries. They have to stop being "lover" and start being a friend. And giving and receiving physical distance is part of that shift.

Distance gives perspective. It helps us see the big picture. It helps us let go of our need to control all the little things. It helps us realize that we are being too aggressive, too intrusive, too judgmental, too controlling toward our partners. It helps us realize that we have crossed the line and need to step back.

Stepping back means that we regain our connection to

our center. We stop looking to our partners to meet our needs in that moment. We see if we can meet those needs directly and, if we can't, we realize that those needs may be false, distorted, unrealistic. And we begin to ask ourselves why we are looking to someone else to give something to us that we are unable to give to ourselves.

We look at our own neurotic need for approval and see how it is unfair to expect our partner to meet that need. We need to learn to validate ourselves. When we can do that, we see that our partners are loving us as well as they can, but they can't fill that black hole in our hearts. Nobody can fill it.

That hole is there because we don't appreciate ourselves. And we have to keep coming back to it: loving and accepting ourselves regardless of how messy or confusing our lives appear.

Nobody is excused from the great work of self-acceptance, especially in the context of an intimate relationship. Indeed, the more intense our relationship is, the more essential it becomes that we take time alone to re-center and love and accept ourselves.

If we give that job to our partners—a possibility that continues to seduce us—we end up betraying ourselves. Our partner's love and acceptance of us can never be a substitute for our love and acceptance of ourselves.

Loving ourselves is the foundation. Our partner's love is carried by the strength of that foundation or undermined by its weakness.

If the foundation is weak, the relationship will self-destruct. It is unable to bear the weight that is put on it.

In any relationship, it is our responsibility to keep our own foundation strong. That means taking good care of ourselves physically, emotionally, mentally and spiritually.

It means taking care of our bodies: eating well, exercising, getting enough sleep. It means taking time to feel, work through, and express our feelings. It means being aware of our thoughts and seeing how they either contribute to our happiness or undermine it. And it means connecting with our Essence on a regular basis.

Yes, that's a lot. But that is what builds the foundation.

If we try to get all of this from our partner, we are bound to be disappointed. It's time to stop trying.

If our partner is able to keep his or her own foundation strong, then s/he is giving us the greatest blessing possible. We don't need more than that. More than that is an illusion.

You can care for your partner, but you cannot help him/her build the foundation of self acceptance and self love. That is individual work.

That is the gift we bring to relationship. Without it, any

relationship is an exercise in futility. As soon as the ground shakes, the foundation will crack and building will come crashing down.

Of course, we must realize that building the foundation is not something we do in five minutes. It is something that requires our constant attention. Even five minutes a day will not suffice.

Periodically, throughout the day, we are called to care for ourselves on many levels. When I consider this in detail, I realize that several hours each day are necessary: time to swim, to walk, to be quiet, to write, and so forth.

It is not a small thing. If I spend four hours a day taking care of myself and honoring my own process, then I have the energy to connect with someone else. If I don't, then I come to my relationship weak and unprepared.

Of course, it is different for each person. But each person must come to terms with what s/he needs to bring the fullness of self into a relationship with another.

I think we seriously underestimate the time and energy that goes into keeping ourselves and our relationships healthy.

How do we structure our lives so that there is time for self, time for our partner, and time for our other commitments? Should we build rituals into our lives that allow us time for self and time for sharing with our partners?

Should we consider having separate living spaces, a room of our own in the house, or perhaps even our own home to retreat to when we need to have time for self-communion, time to be rooted in the rhythms our own experience?

These are the questions we all need to ask.

And we will each find our own answers and live out those answers imperfectly.

At times we will fall flat on our faces and have to get up and make a whole new agreement. That's okay. That's part of the process of learning and growing together. It's all trial and error until we find what works for both of us.

Do not Sing my Praises

"Your love is too much for me now," she said.
"For days I have stood many-hued in the light
of your rising and setting sun.

Now it is time for me to walk into the meadow alone.
It does not matter that all I bring on my return
is a few stones to set at your feet.

What matters is me coming and going,
and you being there when I return.

A woman is more than a moon.
She is a sun too.

She is a gatherer of her own crop.
She is not only the one who holds you,
but the one who feeds you too.

Today, please do not call me or send me flowers.
Do not sing my praises
or tell me how magnificent our union is.

Today I need to sit alone by the stream.
or lay alone in bed
with the covers over my head.

No, I am not hiding from you.
It's just that I have forgotten where my skin ends
and yours begins.

Today, I need to remember who I am apart from you.
How else can I continue to give myself to you?

Today, I need to empty myself of your love
to find my own."

A New Covenant

A relationship is a covenant between two people. It defines what both people are willing to do. It honestly states what each person feels s/he can give freely. It is not a call for mutual sacrifice.

It must not be about what people give up to be together. It must be about what people bring willingly to each other. It must be about what they take pleasure in giving and receiving.

A relationship is not about demands. Once one person begins to demand from the other, the relationship ceases to be. There is no more covenant.

A covenant is not just made once for all time. It is made week by week, day by day, hour by hour, moment by moment.

In this moment, we are either willing or we are not. And if we are not willing to give what we promised to give, then the promise has no meaning.

You cannot make someone do what s/he said s/he was going to do. Coercion is not an aspect of relationship.

Coercion is a sign of lack of relationship.

So what do we do when one person is unwilling? Do we say, "It's okay. I release you from your commitment"?

Or do we say "I have relied on your commitment. Please try to fulfill the agreement you made with me"?

It seems to me that you do not want to be with a person who is unable to be committed to you, regardless of what words s/he uttered in the past.

You do not want to hold onto someone in pain, or you will share in that pain.

You do not want to keep someone against his or her will or you will spend your life battling that resistance.

You cannot make a relationship happen.

A relationship is a covenant. It is an agreement between two people about what they are willing to do.

If only one person is willing, it is not a relationship. It is a form of trespass.

Real love has no possibility to come into its fullness without a true and firm commitment from both people. It doesn't happen between two skittish people. It doesn't happen when two people keep running away from each other.

It happens only when two people learn to stand together. And sometimes that is hard.

Sometimes two people do not know how to stand together. Sometimes, they aren't even sure they want to be together.

This happens in every relationship. Highs become lows. Energy and interest wanes.

Sex is no longer emotionally fulfilling. Talking to each other seems difficult.

Within every relationship, there are moments of non-relationship. Smart couples use these moments to take time alone to reconnect with self and to recharge.

They don't end their relationship when the energy gets low. They don't have an affair.

They give each other room to breathe.

It might be for an hour or two, for a day or two. . . perhaps even for a month or two.

Each person must find ways back into Self and that means disentangling from other.

Each person must find time to ask the question "Who am I now?"

The answer to this question changes from time to time. That is why we must not forget to ask the question.

Relationship is both a journey into intimacy with another and a journey into intimacy with Self. We forget that.

We think it's all about other, but that is not true. Indeed, if our journey into another's heart does not take us into our own, then our progress on the path is interrupted.

We need time to internalize. We need time to breathe and be alone.

It is part of the cycle.

We move together and apart. If we do not move apart, we cannot come back together.

You can't have a relationship with all highs and no lows. You can't have a relationship that is all together.

Every relationship must fall apart, not just once but many times. That is how it grows. That is how new intimacy is achieved.

Our models of relationship don't allow for this kind of interpersonal transformation within the context of a committed relationship. In our models, people either stay together in a frozen state, or they remain distant and uncommitted.

People who stay together "no matter what" stop growing. They cannot even look at each other any more. Life energy leaves the relationship. It cannot abide the limiting patterns and structures.

People who fear intimacy take a rocketship out of the relationship at the first sign of trouble. They move from lover to lover, never breaking through to the source of love, in themselves or in the other person.

Some relationships have no staying power. Others have no transforming power.

Real relationships require both. They require commitment to each other and freedom to be ourselves. They ask us to keep telling the truth as we move together through our sadness and pain.

Successful relationships require that we have the strength

to stand our ground when it is necessary and the flexibility to adapt when circumstances change. Sometimes they ask us to wait patiently. Sometimes they ask us to move forward energetically, even though we aren't sure where we are going.

No relationship is easy. Each intimate relationship tests the depth of our commitment to ourselves and others. Gradually, in the crucible of relationship, selfish love dies and is reborn as love without conditions.

This transcendent, agape love that remains throughout the highs and lows of our emotional experience does not blossom all at once. It is a gradual ripening. It unfolds more deeply each time we meet our partner in the circle. Greeting and letting go, embracing and releasing: these are the tides of love. There is no heart that does not know them.

The beauty of the dance reveals itself to us when we realize that the very act of letting go of our partner's hand is an invitation to take it once again. Then, when we meet again in the circle, it will be with a greater sense of appreciation and reverence. Our hearts will be more open and welcoming and we will gaze more deeply than ever before into each other's eyes.

Black Ice by the River

How many lovers fall
on the same patch of ice?

On the way there,
in a single moment of inattention,
my legs fly out from under me.

On the way back,
while looking carefully for the dangerous spot,
you go spinning.

Some would say: "It is an omen.
God is telling you to be careful."
I don't think so.

If God is talking, S/he is saying:

"No matter how much care
you take or do not take,
you will still land on your back.

You can't avoid hurt.
You can't avoid embarrassment.
Listen, both of you.

There will be times
when you try to control
and you will fail.

But it is no big deal.
Part of walking together
is falling together.

Part of being in the right relationship
is knowing that you are dead wrong
about each other.

Unless both of you are vulnerable,
imperfect, mistaken, and willing
to be so, it cannot work.

Let go of any idea you have about being right.
Let go of all your pictures of
'the way it should be.'

Just put one foot in front of the other
and walk together in compassion.
Be gentle and forgiving.

Keep setting aside your thoughts.
Keep falling into your heart.
Keep following the river.

Nothing else means anything."

Riverwalk

1

I notice how you immediately go
to where the mountain brook
empties into the river.

In the spring sun, the melting snow
shines and sparkles
on its downward journey.

You watch closely as the tumbling water
creates its own unique path
through the icefalls.

2

Climbing from stone to stone,
we claim the great rock throne
around which the waters rush,

an island in mid-stream,

a place of perfect balance
between movement and stillness,
rootedness and freedom.

Stretching out in the sun,
as the great drone of rushing water
sings to our cells,

we have become a mere ornament
of the hour,
an unexpected flourish,

like the spray that catches the sunlight
at the right moment,

a moment of grace
only briefly noted
as the river rushes past us.

3

Something surrendered to create

this deep depression in the ground,
this nadir into which the melting snow falls
from every surrounding ridge.

I celebrate that which made itself empty
and plunged into the void
so this river could run here.

I celebrate the stillness
that brings the rushing water
and the cries of the raven and the hawk.

I celebrate that emptiness in each of us
and the anointed ones
who answer its call.

Cradled in the Mystery

The sweetness of the river calls to me
where it bends away from the road.

I follow its rising crescendo
beyond human sounds,
taking the first footpath
up into the mountain.

Looking down,
I see the rushing waters
bend beyond sight
catching the last rays of light
as the sun disappears into the next valley.

I am a seeker of wild places,
yet this wilderness between us
is sharper than the edge of night
that closes in around the river.

Once intimidated by it,
I have come here to learn from it
and be reconciled to it.

All through the night
I hear the drumming of the waters,
bringing day back ever so slowly,
like some mystical birth of consciousness
cradled in the mystery.

It is hard for me to admit,
but I do not know the way back to you.
All I know is that we cannot meet
unless we follow the river
into these wild places of the heart,

beyond promises and guarantees,
beyond what we know
or think we know,

where the fire burns relentlessly
and strange shadows dance
in and out of the flames.

Journeys in Place

The morning after you leave to fly back
arrives soft, wispy,
white on white,
floating inside
its unsteady cradle.

Sun begins low in the sky,
warming the waters
that twist in the nadir of earth.
Fog envelopes the valley.
soft, ephemeral,
finding every nook and cranny.

Driving south through the rolling hills
where I-91 slashes through farms
hugging the edge of the Deerfield River,
patches of fog rise slowly,
sweeping ghostlike
over the snowy fields.

The morning sun is
diffused, barely permeating
the vaporous shroud

as it rises up toward the clouds
that linger over the Pocumtuck Ridge.

I do not know if it is the fog,
the sunlight,
or the alchemy of their union
that makes this
wraith-like embrace,

obscuring farmhouse and barn
and blurring the headlights of cars
speeding north along this corridor
once only traveled
by wind and snow.

II

I too used to run with the wind
before love caught my lifted foot
and half-buried it
like a recalcitrant root
in the snow.

Now my eyes peeking out of fog
question even that moment
of forced surrender.

Held in this brief, ephemeral embrace,
(my body still cradled by your hands)
I watch as the rays of sunlight implode,
setting the valley ablaze
in opaque white light.

III

The land stretches out before me
like the body of a lover
I have touched before:

I see the inundations:
the hills and valleys,
and I hear the rustling of the leaves
that fell before death stumbled in
and took the memory
from my hands.

IV

Ravaged in her beauty,
yet strangely compliant,
earth lifts her soft breast
to the lips that seek it.
Any lips. Any time.

Without spilling
a single drop of blood
the wound remains,
echoing thousands of times
as cars speed by.

There is no sensation
where tires tread,
no breath under the road
where the land rises and falls,
no more farms
rolling uninterrupted
down to the river.

Tender Mercies

After you left, I felt your absence poignantly, as I knew I would. You had the same experience, but it was a total surprise for you.

You began to value our relationship in a whole new way. You allowed yourself to sink more deeply into our friendship. You let my love in.

But it was too late.

I kept making plans to come and see you, but those plans didn't materialize. There was no energy in my life supporting my movement in your direction.

When you walked out of the door of this house something shifted. And, in time, another door opened.

It opened spontaneously and without effort and I walked through it. I know that you wouldn't have done it. You would have waited, analyzed the situation, considered whether or not your needs were going to be met.

But none of this occurred to me. For the first time in my life love was offered to me as I have offered it to others. There were no conditions to meet. There was just a simple uncomplicated "yes."

The purity of the gesture, and the integrity that stood behind it, made it absolutely compelling. It left no room for doubt or deliberation.

It was not a gesture that you could respond to half-heartedly or ambivalently. It required your total presence and commitment.

Of course, you never liked that "C" word. For you, it represented a loss of freedom.

But that was because you understood commitment as something that would be extracted from you, almost against your will. You did not realize that such a commitment could not exist without your willingness to offer it.

In truth, our potential for committed love is universal, but we don't trust it. We are afraid of being betrayed.

We live in our heads and think love to death. We consider every problem. We examine every pimple and wart. We expect perfection and forget to offer forgiveness to ourselves or others.

When we trust, love is a fountain of promise and a river of hope. We move easily in the changing currents of the river. When we distrust, we erect an inner barrier that damns up the flow of emotion and makes it difficult for us to give and receive spontaneously. By dwelling on our doubts and fears and asking for guarantees, we impede the natural rhythm of life.

Without trust in ourselves and our partners, the dance becomes difficult. Some of us get frustrated and retreat from the dance floor feeling angry or victimized. Yet our isolation and unhappiness are of our own making.

When we listen to our fears, refuse to take risks, and try to control the outcome of every situation, our minds are falsely empowered. They strip the heart of its authority and preside over a shadowy kingdom of their own creation.

Meanwhile the heart languishes in its prison.

A heart that is not given permission to love is a sorry thing. It has no power to go beyond itself. It loses both the connection to its roots and the reach of its wings.

The great poet and painter William Blake portrayed this artificial dominance of the head over the heart in the character of *Urizen*. He showed us a figure with a huge head and a diminutive body. His unsightly vision has become the dominant reality of contemporary life. It is essentially perverse and neurotic.

A heart that does not reach out and risk is bound and shackled in its prison of fear until it has the courage to trust again. But its bravery will pay off. When the heart rises up and takes its power back, balance is restored and the prison door swings open.

Love may be born in the shadows, but it is not a shadowy thing. It is a bright, radiant creature that celebrates life and rises like the Phoenix from the ashes of its pain and disappointment.

It is a creature that lives on trust, hope and faith. It

gives of itself unselfishly, in spite of all the fears that conspire to hold it back.

It was never meant to be confined and imprisoned, but to be free to experience all of the highs and lows of human emotion. In this respect, pain, hurt, and sadness are inevitable. All who dance passionately experience both joy and sorrow.

To refuse to dance because of the risk of injury is to discount the heart and reject the promise of love. It is a sterile choice. And in the end it does not deliver the safety that it promises.

The Cup

When you said you found my love
overwhelming,
I dimmed my light
and curtailed my passion
to fit the size of your cup.

But I must ask you:
Why not stretch a little?
Why not make yourself
a little deeper and wider
so that you can contain
all the love I have to give?

Isn't this the kind of yoga
lovers must learn to do,
shrinking and expanding
until they can finally go
beyond themselves?

I am sorry, my friend.
You may believe
that the cup of love
gets smaller,
but it isn't true.

It may get smashed, demolished,
recycled and reshaped,
but its capacity to give
or to receive
never becomes less than it is.

The Well

Whenever I think that
it is not possible for me to love you
more than I do in this moment,
it soon becomes clear
that this is not true.

The well we draw from
is deeper than we know.

The Heroic Journey

We all want to merge into something greater than ourselves. That is the fiat of love.

We aspire to go beyond ourselves, to overcome our separateness. But, in order to do so, we must give up the ways in which we hold ourselves in and back. We must give up the very boundaries that we have always looked to for self-definition.

An insecure person cannot do this. S/he needs those boundaries to feel safe.

Love isn't something that happens when we are fearful or insecure. Because love means taking a risk. It means reaching out with the possibility that we will be denied or rejected. It means crossing over our safe zone and becoming vulnerable.

The movement of love offers a new engagement with life, a new possibility for growth and transformation.

Love puts us right out on a limb. It is exciting. We see things we have never seen before. But it is scary too.

Love is the movement from the core of self to the periphery. Love expands our sense of self to include others.

When we love, we become bigger. Our little soap opera reaches epic proportions.

As lover, we become a mythic figure: not just man or woman, but god or goddess. Love helps us step into our divinity.

When we love, all this great energy stands behind us, supporting and encouraging us, pushing us forward.

How, in the midst of this great energetic phenomenon, does fear manage to get a foothold? How is it able to twist and turn the natural spontaneity and expressiveness of love inward, making the creative neurotic and self-absorbed?

Of course, the great fear of the lover is that his love will not be requited. He will not be loved back as much as he loves. Indeed, his love may be spurned!

If he worries about this, he cannot love. Fearing rejection, he never takes the risk of letting his love be known.

If we are afraid of failure, rejection or looking foolish, we cannot love. That is because love is, after all, completely foolish.

Anyone who has been stuck by Cupid's arrow will attest to the fact that foolishness is the mark of love.

The question is not "what would love do?'

The question is "what would love not do?"

Love will not hold back. It will completely embarrass and compromise itself in its need to make itself known.

Where is the lover who is restrained in his expression of love? You won't find him.

Love may know excess, but it does not know restraint.

The one who loves must be willing to play the fool. He must be willing to embarrass himself. He must be willing to make mistakes. He must be willing to love even though there is no guarantee he will be loved back.

If he is not willing, fear will turn his energy back. He will seek safety and guarantees. He will contract.

His chance to become greater than himself will cease to be. His opportunity to become heroic will pass.

For what love can do, fear can undo.

There is no way around it.

Though fear is powerless in the face of love, love's power cannot be experienced as long as we listen to our fears.

Fear says "no." Love says "yes."

Fear says "it can be done only this way." Love says "it can be done in any way it needs to be done."

All life is a poem about separation and joining. Fear separates. Love unites.

We aren't going to make fear go away. It's part of the dualistic fabric of life.

We just need to learn how to hold it. When we can hold our fear in a loving way, it no longer has the power to undermine us.

Fears come up, but we don't assume that our fears are true. Nor do we try to make them go away. We just allow them to be held spaciously in consciousness.

When we hold our fears lovingly, there can be no neurotic, knee jerk reactions. We don't have to abandon our lovers at the first sign of difficulty.

We can acknowledge our fears without embellishing them or falsely empowering them. That way we never give them the power to turn our love back on itself.

When our fears have been acknowledged, the space in consciousness opens up again. We stop being contracted. We just let things be. And in this open space, love is rediscovered.

We don't have to try and turn fear around. We don't have to try to make fear go away.

Fear does not have to be opposed. It needs to be held compassionately.

Fear only holds us back if we let it: if we believe it at face value, or if we are afraid of it and try to push it away. But if we meet our fear compassionately, it is no problem. It is like the wind picking up before a storm and dying down after it. It comes and goes.

In a life of love, there is room for fear to come and go. And whether coming or going, it does not stop the lover from loving or the beloved from receiving love.

Those who cannot love or receive love because of their fears need to stop listening to their fears.

It's that simple.

They can justify those fears, put them up on an altar and worship them, but they will just be taking themselves further and further away from the Source of love.

Only when they start loving in spite of their fears will they turn the page on an old story and open to new one free of the pain of the past.

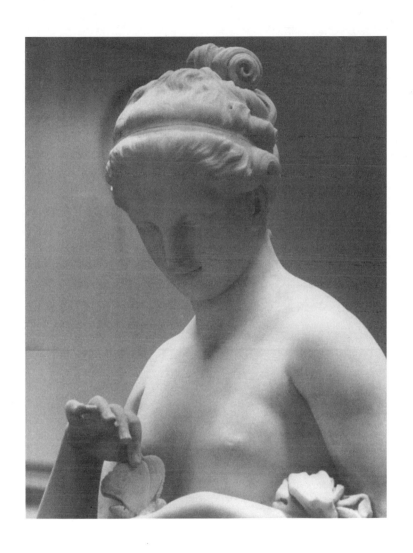

The Falls

Except for a few moments of forgetfulness,
we move in the container of our love
as the river moves in the riverbed.

River of Life

What does it mean: to move in the container of our love?

It means that our love is greater than we are. It is bigger and stronger than we can ever be. It has the capacity to contain us even as we vacillate from one thought/feeling state to another.

Our love is like a mother or father on whom we can rely to keep us safe. It holds us gently, regardless of what is happening in our lives.

It is like the riverbed that has been made over thousands of years by the natural flow of water to its lowest point. Just as the river makes the riverbed and then moves within it, love makes us its container so that it can express through us.

We do not know why we love each other. We just know with a certainty that it is so.

People try to rationalize love. They try to break it down into its component elements. They say that love is born of physical attraction, shared values and interests. Yet people may be attracted to each other and share each other's interests and values and still not fall in love.

Or they may fall in love for a month or two and then fall out of love again.

But people who share a great love—people who are truly stronger together than they are apart—will tell you that there is nothing reasonable or even optional about their love for each other.

Love for them was never a choice. It was and continues to be an immediate necessity.

When you know something to be true, deliberation is not necessary. The choice is so clear it does not seem like a choice at all.

Truth, after all, is not divided. It is completely whole and indivisible. When true love comes into our life, we have no need to analyze the situation. We know exactly what to say and do.

There is no need even for thought.

Love does not require persuasion or convincing. It is an absolute fiat. It is a law unto itself.

Those who are seized by the power of love cannot but surrender to it. They are powerless to oppose it, because they have joined with it totally.

How can you oppose that with which you are joined?

It is not possible.

Others may seek to interfere with or pull apart what love has joined, but they will not be successful. Nothing can obstruct or impede that which is effortlessly true. And that which is not fabricated cannot be pulled apart.

It is a gift of the universe. And once the gift has been given and received, it cannot be taken back.

As Rumi says: lovers do not just meet somewhere. They are in each other all along.

Their meeting is merely a recognition of what they know has always been true.

Remember, it is not hard for the river to move in the riverbed. It is completely easy and natural.

The only time it becomes difficult is in times of great draught or flood, times when there is too little or too much emotion. And, at such times, the shape of the riverbed may change to accommodate the increase or decrease in energy.

When we love truly, it is not hard to stay in our love. All it requires is a deep breath, a sigh, a relaxing into what is. All it requires is a sinking into the arms that hold us.

When you love, loving is not complicated. It is not even difficult.

It is complicated and difficult only when you don't love.

Then, you think it requires a lot of work because you are trying to force yourself or another to love.

But force is not part of the language of love. Force is a sign that love is absent.

Force pushes the river over its banks. It destroys the farms that lie along both sides of the river.

That is why the lover must be able to surrender, not just

once, but thousands of times. He must surrender his own will to the greater Will. He must surrender his own selfish desires to the greater needs of the relationship.

This surrender is not work. It is a relaxation.

It is yielding up of all that is not whole to that which is whole. It is a trust in the river itself.

Each day the lover surrenders to love as the river surrenders to the riverbank. And each day the lover is carried by the current of love to whatever destination love requires.

He does not know where he is going. Indeed, he knows that he has no choice.

He has stopped trying to choose for himself.

He has learned to let love choose for him.

And his beloved does the same, not because he asks it of her, but because she too has surrendered to love.

When two surrender to love, their relationship is effortless and full of grace. They both have the same changeless goal and they know that the way to reach it will be provided.

Trust is required from both of them for such a love to bloom. Yet they cannot in any way influence who the beloved is or when s/he comes. They can merely recognize the beloved when s/he stands before them.

No vows are necessary for those who mutually acknowledge the beloved in each other. Their love for each other is itself the proclamation of a commitment made in their hearts and it will be witnessed by all who come to know them.

The surrender to life necessarily precedes the creation of true relationship, because only those who know how to surrender to life can surrender to each other.

Baptism by Fire

Narcissus got wet trying to embrace
his image in the water.

When I look into your eyes,
all images of self or other
explode into flames.

When the fire abates,
the Phoenix rises
from the ashes left behind.

It is not you or I,
yet it moves with our legs
and calls out with our voice.

A Third Body

Lovers give birth to a third body.
Its lungs have the capacity
to breathe for two,
although they breathe something
other than air.
Its heart has the strength
to keep two alive,
although it pumps something
other than blood.

This body is not made of flesh,
but of thought and feeling.
It is the labor of two hearts
and two minds
that have learned
to dance together.

Although it is created by two
who live in separate bodies,
those two
inhabit this body
they have made together
when those separate bodies die.

Haiku

You have taken me there:
into that river of light
fluttering under the leaves.

Fear of Surrender

We are afraid to surrender to the beloved because we do not trust ourselves.

We are afraid to give another person power over us, because we do not have faith in our own power.

It seems that we are afraid to love another. But the truth is we are afraid to love ourselves.

We seek validation in the other, but such external validation is impossible. It can only come from within.

Without that self-validation, it is impossible to love anyone else.

If one feels inferior or superior to others, one can be sure that self-validation is missing.

Self-validation makes the extension of love possible.

Love is possible only when you and I both know that we are worthy.

Then there is no sacrifice in our loving. And, if there is no sacrifice, then love cannot be neurotic. It cannot be distorted or turned back upon itself.

What is given can be received and given in return. Mutuality prevails.

The relationship is properly polarized so that current moves back and forth between the two poles.

For proper polarization, each pole must be intact. In a

dynamic relationship, each partner must be self validated and whole in him or herself.

Each must be confident. Each must be worthy. Each must be willing to give and receive love.

Self trust is essential for trust of others. Self love is necessary for love of others. Self confidence is necessary for confidence in others.

We cannot find outside of us what does not already exist within.

If you need another person's love or attention to be strong, then your strength is an illusion.

If you need to dominate others to feel good about yourself, then you self-worth is paper thin.

Neither a leech nor a tyrant is capable of real love. The only love they know is co-dependent and abusive to self and other.

Who are the people who are most successful in relationship? They are the ones who have learned to love and trust themselves and are ready to extend the same blessing to others.

They are confident, but not cocky or selfish. Their strength is within. That is why they are able to be gentle with others.

The Seventh Day

I

You take six days
to realize
that you don't like
being invaded.

On the seventh day,
you go on the warpath;
can't even stand
the sound of his voice.

The man you say
you want to spend your life with
has become your arch enemy.
So much for your romantic fantasies!

They have given you
an irregular heartbeat,
and left him wandering
the streets of the city at dawn.

II

Angelic creatures without wings
have their arms and legs broken,
their hearts wrought into a fury
by dragons rising up from below.

Now, you know

there are many small deaths
before the mind stops clinging
and surrenders to the final chaos
beyond thought.

III

You want to embrace the divine
without touching the turmoil
in your heart.

It is not possible.

IV

Some people pretend to be okay,
while in their minds
they constantly relive
their feelings of violation.

But sooner or later
the volcano erupts,
and the flow of molten rock
destroys everything in its path.

V

All that meticulous work,
destroyed in a day
when the dark river
comes crashing in.

River of night
flowing through the heart
red with the blood
of dragons slain.

River of tears,
flowing to its final resting place,
the deep black sea
of acceptance,

where everything is as it is,
and cannot be denied,
hidden, exaggerated or imposed
on anything else.

Acceptance

Since relationship cannot be forced, we need to pay attention to what works spontaneously, without deliberation or effort.

We may want a relationship to work, but that does not mean that it will work.

To be sure, mutual willingness and a shared vision increase the odds of success in a relationship, but there is another factor that is equally important.

It is the way two people naturally interact together physically, emotionally, mentally, and spiritually. Some people call it "chemistry." But often this term refers to the kind of sexual charge in a relationship and, as such, it does not reflect the kind of ease and familiarity people feel in each other's presence in non-sexual ways.

What I am talking about here is not just a sexual connection, but a coherence of energies on all levels, the physical manifestations of which include enjoying the other person's smell and touch, wanting to look into his or her eyes, feeling uplifted by the sound of his or her voice. It is a "whole body" or "full sensual" chemistry.

It extends to the way we walk and talk with this person. We feel at ease. We feel that we complement each other.

We appreciate and admire each other naturally. We

don't have to work at it. It just happens as a matter of course.

A relationship like this is a gift of the universe.

It is an ongoing blessing.

We don't have to work to obtain it or maintain it. All we have to do is to be ourselves and do our part.

In such a relationship, it never occurs to us to act in a selfish or self-protective way. We don't withhold our love or support. We give generously without thinking about "me" or "mine." We are content to share all that we have.

When the other person needs something, it gives us great pleasure to meet that need.

The good and well-being of our partner is as important as our own good and well-being.

This is not something that we "try" to do. It is our natural inclination.

Whenever we have to "try" to love someone, we can be sure that we aren't anywhere close to being loving.

Love expresses itself spontaneously. It requires no planning, no practice, no effort.

So much for "making love." It's impossible. Love cannot be "made."

It is a gift that is given to us. And we have no choice but to pass it on.

No, we don't make love. Love makes us.

Love smoothes our rough edges. It softens us and helps us open our hearts.

Love holds us and keeps us. It shows us how to lie down in green pastures. It restores our soul to us.

Love is our teacher and our guide.

We cannot make ourselves love others. We cannot make others love us.

But we can ask love to teach us and guide us.

We can ask love to remove the obstacles we place before it.

We can get out of the way and let love do what it needs to do.

We can stop relying on ourselves and begin the process of surrender. We can start to rely on love, allowing it to dissolve our resistance and remake us in its image.

This is not cosmetic surgery, but soul surgery. It is absolute reconstruction.

It is a tearing down of the false and a revelation of the essence. It is a rebuilding of the house of life with the light and grace of truth.

Only if our ego structure is dismantled and our self-confidence rebuilt by Spirit are we able to love in an unselfish way.

Unless we undergo this reconstruction process, we will not be ready to serve the beloved when s/he comes to us.

Can you imagine telling the beloved for whom you have waited all your life: "Excuse me, but I'm not quite ready. Can you come back next week or next month?"

You don't turn the beloved down.

You bow and say "Namaste. It is an honor to meet you."

You don't say: "I'm not ready to dance. I'm still taking lessons."

You say: "Please forgive my clumsiness. What I lack in skill I will make up for in willingness."

When the invitation to dance comes, you have no choice but to say "Yes. Thank you."

All your life you have been waiting for this moment. How can you hesitate? How can you consider asking love to await your perceived readiness?

I will tell you this. Love does not come to you until you are ready.

It doesn't matter whether you feel ready or not. Love knows.

Love knows when the time to dance has come. And it always arrives at the right time.

So, be humble, my friend. The timing of the invitation is not up to you.

All you can do is keep surrendering, keep getting out of the way, keep letting love guide you and shape you.

And then the invitation will come. Perhaps it will come

when you sense it will. Perhaps it will come when you least expect it.

No matter.

Your job is not to try to control who the beloved is or when s/he comes. Your job is simply to recognize the beloved when s/he stands before you.

And once you do, the person you once were will be annihilated. The "you" that has always kept separate and apart will be destroyed.

There will be nothing that stands between you and the beloved. Because you and the beloved will become one person, one energy, one unified vision and goal.

This is what is means to be Christed, to go beyond the separate sense of self, to join in the oneness of creation.

If you can do this with one person, you can do it with all. That is why sacred marriage is the doorway to love without conditions.

No one can make this happen.

You can't decide to annihilate the ego. The ego merely falls away when you have no more use for it.

When you are ready to honor the beloved, he or she arrives. And then there are no more separate agendas, separate wants, separate goals.

There is only one agenda, one desire, one goal. And that is to be an instrument of love.

"Lord, allow me to be an instrument of your love, your acceptance, your compassion."

That is what St. Francis asked for.

That is what each of us asks for when the beloved comes.

May you all be blessed.

May you find the essence within and without. May you find the inner bride/groom and the outer one.

May you dance with faith. May you dance with confidence. May you dance as you have never danced before.

Prayer

May you rest in my love
as the river rests in the river bed,

as the hawk rests in the updraft of air
that carries him up above the mountain.

May your lows deepen me.
May your highs stretch me.

May you lean against me
when your burden is heavy

and find sanctuary in my arms
when you lose your way home.

May my softness comfort you.
May my firmness support you.

May you rest in my love
as the great ones rest in the eternal Tao,

as the wise ones rest
in the certainty of God.

The Certainty of Your Love

Now that I live in the certainty of your love,
I am no longer charmed by beauty's promise
or wisdom's gain.

Ancient jewels no longer sparkle,
nor do sacred scrolls sing in my sight.

What more is there to gain in the world?
Only your love sets me free.
Anything else is a ball and a chain.

The Meeting

I always knew that you would come to me
and that I would recognize you
when you came.

I knew I would see myself
When I looked into your eyes
and feel your heart beating
when I took your hand in mine.

You see, you are no stranger to me.
I have known you
for a very long time,

and now, through some extraordinary grace
· I cannot begin to understand,
you stand before me.

I greet you, my dear one.
I celebrate this meeting of inner and outer,
of heart and mind,
body and spirit.

All that has been separate and apart
has now come back together.
Two have become one.

Heaven and earth are joined.
Human and divine are touching.
What has always been true
is true now in us.

We give thanks.
May that which blesses us
bless all beings.

Paul Ferrini is the author of over 40 books on love, healing and forgiveness. His unique blend of spirituality and psychology goes beyond self-help and recovery into the heart of healing. His conferences, retreats, and *Affinity Group Process* have helped thousands of people deepen their practice of forgiveness and open their hearts to the divine presence in themselves and others.

For more information on Paul's work, visit the website at *www.paulferrini.com*. The website has many excerpts from Paul Ferrini's books, as well as information on his workshops and retreats. Be sure to request Paul's free email newsletter, as well as a free catalog of his books and audio products. You can also email: info@**heartwayspress.com** or write to **Heartways Press, 9 Phillips Steet, Greenfield, MA 01301.**

New Audio Releases

Being an Instrument of Love in Times of Planetary Crisis
Two Talks on Individual and Collective Healing

2 CDs $24.95   ISBN 978-1-879159-79-2

The Radiant Light Within
Readings by Paul Ferrini from the Hidden Jewel &
Dancing with the Beloved
1 CD $16.95   ISBN 978-1-879159-74-7

Real Happiness
Awakening To Our True Self
An Introductory Talk by Paul Ferrini
1 CD $16.95   ISBN 978-1-879159-75-4

Roadmap to Real Happiness
Living the Life of Joy and Purpose
You Were Meant to Live   Part 1
4 CDs $48.00   ISBN 978-1-879159-72-3

Part 2   3 CDs $36.00
ISBN 978-1-879159-73-0

Creating a Life of Fulfillment
Insights on Work, Relationship and Life Purpose
2 CDs $24.95
ISBN 978-1-879159-76-1

Paul Ferrini's Course in Spiritual Mastery

Part One: The Laws of Love
A Guide to Living in Harmony
with Universal Spiritual Truth
144 pages $12.95
ISBN # 1-879159-60-0

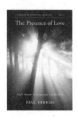

Part Two: The Power of Love
10 Spiritual Practices that Can Transform Your Life
168 pages $12.95
ISBN # 1-879159-61-9

Part Three: The Presence of Love
God's Answer to Humanity's Call for Help
160 pages $12.95
ISBN # 1-879159-62-7

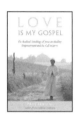

Part Four: Love is My Gospel
The Radical Teachings of Jesus on Healing,
Empowerment and the Call to Serve
128 pages $12.95
ISBN # 1-879159-67-8

Part Five: Real Happiness

A Roadmap for Healing Our Pain and Awakening
the Joy That Is Our Birthright
160 pages $12.95
ISBN # 978-1-879159-68-6

Part Six: Embracing Our True Self

A New Paradigm Approach to Healing Our Wounds,
Finding Our Gifts, and Fulfilling Our Spiritual
Purpose
192 pages $13.95
ISBN # 978-1-879159-69-3

Part Seven: Real Happiness— The Workbook

Creating Your Personal Roadmap
to a Joyful and Empowered Life
96 pages $14.95
ISBN # 978-1-879159-71-6

Paul's In-depth Presentation of the Laws of Love on 9 CDs

THE LAWS OF LOVE

Part One (5 CDs) ISBN # 1-879159-58-9 $49.00
Part Two (4 CDs) ISBN # 1-879159-59-7 $39.00

Paul Ferrini's Real Happiness Workshop

By Real Happiness we mean the ability to be true to ourselves, kind to others, and able to weather the ups and downs of life with acceptance and compassion.

This powerful workshop is designed to help us learn to love and accept ourselves radically and profoundly. Participants will learn to:

- Accept, nurture and bring love to themselves.

- Be true to themselves and live honestly and authentically.

- Make and accept responsibility for their own decisions.

- Discover their talents/gifts and find their passion/purpose.

- Cultivate an open heart and an open mind.

- Forgive and learn from their mistakes.

- Be patient with the process of healing and transformation.

- Cultivate a positive attitude toward life and see obstacles as challenges.

- Develop the capacity to hear their inner guidance and surrender to their spiritual purpose.

A genuinely happy person lives in *Right Relationship* to self and others and engages in *Right Livelihood,* expressing his or her gifts and bringing joy to self and others. These are therefore the goals of this work. For more information about how you can bring this workshop to your community call us at 1-888-HARTWAY.

Audio Workshops on CD

Seeds of Transformation:
Set includes: Healing Without Fixing, The Wound and the Gift, Opening to the Divine Love Energy, The Laws of Love, The Path to Mastery.
5 CDs   ISBN 1-879159-63-5 $48.00

Two Talks on Spiritual Mastery
by Paul Ferrini
We are the Bringers of Love   CD 1
Surrendering to What Is   CD 2
2 CDs   ISBN 1-879159-65-1 $24.00

Love is That Certainty
ISBN 1-879159-52-X $16.95

Atonement:
The Awakening of Planet Earth and its Inhabitants
ISBN 1-879159-53-8 $16.95

From Darkness to Light:
The Soul's Journey of Redemption
ISBN 1-879159-54-6 $16.95

Relationship Books

Dancing with the Beloved:
Opening our Hearts to the Lessons of Love
ISBN 1-879159-47-3
160 pages paperback $12.95

Living in the Heart:
The Affinity Process and the Path of Unconditional
Love and Acceptance
128 pages   paperback   ISBN 1-879159-36-8
$10.95

Creating a Spiritual Relationship
128 pages   paperback
ISBN 1-879159-39-2 $10.95

The Twelve Steps of Forgiveness
120 pages   paperback   ISBN 1-879159-10-4
$10.95

The Ecstatic Moment:
A Practical Manual for Opening Your Heart
and Staying in It
128 pages   paperback   ISBN 1-879159-18-X
$10.95

Christ Mind Books and Audio

 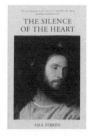 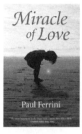 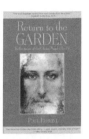

Part 1   Part 2   Part 3   Part 4

   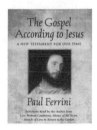

Christ Mind Books

Love Without Conditions ISBN 1-879159-15-5 $12.95

The Silence of the Heart ISBN 1-879159-16-3 $14.95

Miracle of Love ISBN 1-879159-23-6 $12.95

Return to the Garden ISBN 1-879159-35-x $12.95

The Living Christ ISBN 1-879159-49-X paperback $14.95

I am the Door hardcover ISBN 1-879159-41-4 $21.95

The Way of Peace hardcover ISBN 1-879159-42-2 $19.95

Christ Mind Audio Read by the Author

Love Without Conditions
3 CDs ISBN 978-1-879159-64-8 $36.00

The Gospel According to Jesus Selected Readings from the
Christ Mind Teachings 2CDs ISBN 978-1-879159-78-5 $24.95

Wisdom Books and Audio

Everyday Wisdom
A Spiritual Book of Days
224 pages paperback $13.95
ISBN 1-879159-51-1

Wisdom Cards:
Spiritual Guidance for Every Day of our Lives
ISBN 1-879159-50-3 $10.95
*Each full color card features a beautiful
painting evoking an archetypal theme*

Forbidden Fruit:
Unraveling the Mysteries of Sin, Guilt
and Atonement
ISBN 1-879159-48-1
160 pages paperback $12.95

Enlightenment for Everyone
with an Introduction by Iyanla Vanzant
ISBN 1-879159-45-7
160 pages hardcover $16.00

The Great Way of All Beings:
Renderings of Lao Tzu
ISBN 1-879159-46-5
320 pages hardcover $23.00

Grace Unfolding:
The Art of Living A Surrendered Life
96 pages   paperback   ISBN 1-879159-37-6 $9.95

Illuminations on the Road to Nowhere
160 pages   paperback
ISBN 1-879159-44-9 $12.95

Audio Books

The Economy of Love Readings from *Silence of the Heart, The Ecstatic Moment, Grace Unfolding* and other books.
ISBN 1-879159-56-2 $16.95

Relationship as a Spiritual Path Readings from *Creating a Spiritual Relationship, Dancing with the Beloved, Miracle of Love* and other books. ISBN 1-879159-55-4 $16.95

The Hands of God Readings from *Illuminations, Enlightenment for Everyone, Forbidden Fruit, The Great Way of All Beings* and other books. ISBN 1-879159-57-0 $16.95

Heart and Soul Poems of Love and Awakening read by the Author.
ISBN 978-1-879159-77-8   1 CD $16.95

Heartways Press Order Form

Name _____

Address_____

City _____State _____Zip_____

Phone/Fax_____ Email* _____

Please include your email to receive Paul's newsletter and weekly wisdom message.

Title ordered	quantity	price

TOTAL _____

Priority Shipping: one book $5.95   _____

Additional books, please add $1 per book   _____

TOTAL _____

For shipping outside the USA, or if you require rush shipping,
please contact us for shipping costs

Send Order To: Heartways Press 9 Phillips Street,
Greenfield, MA 01301   413-774-9474
Toll free: 1-888-HARTWAY (Orders only)
www.PaulFerrini.com   email: info@heartwayspress.com

Please allow 1–2 weeks for delivery. Payment must be made by check or credit card (MC/VISA/AmEx) before books are shipped. Please make out your check or money order (U.S. funds only) to Heartways Press.